Endorphin Angels

Acknowledgements:

Thanks are due to the editors of the following publications, in which some of these poems have appeared: *Hearts and Minds* 1994, *Poetry West Anthology* 1992, *The Rialto*, *Westwords* 1990.

'Signs': prize winner, Bridport International Poetry Competition 2000.
'Holding On': commended, Arvon/Daily Telegraph Poetry Competition 1999.
'Blue': second prize, Peterloo Poetry Competition 1998.
'Reflection in a Photograph': commissioned by HTV for the 'Freezeframe' series. Poetry prize in the Progetto Omero Poetry Competition for Turin Cultural Festival 1997. Prize winning poem in English and Italian, anthologised in *La Faccia Obscura della Luna* (*The Dark Side of the Moon*).
'Where does the Dark Go?': prize winner, Sidmouth Poetry Festival 1990.

Endorphin Angels was the overall winner in The Poetry Business Book & Pamphlet Competition 2000

Endorphin Angels

Dennis Casling

Smith/Doorstop Books

Published 2001 by
Smith/Doorstop Books
The Poetry Business
The Studio
Byram Arcade
Westgate
Huddersfield HD1 1ND

Copyright © Dennis Casling 2001
All Rights Reserved

Dennis Casling hereby asserts his moral right to be identified as the author of this book.

ISBN 1-902382-32-3

British Library Cataloguing-in-Publication Data. A catalogue record for this book is available from the British Library.

Typeset at The Poetry Business
Printed by Peepal Tree Press, Leeds

Cover photograph: 'Church Window' © Michèle Powell

Smith/Doorstop are represented by Signature Book Representation Ltd, 2 Little Peter Street, Manchester M15 4PS, and distributed by Littlehampton Book Services Ltd.

The Poetry Business gratefully acknowledges the help of Kirklees Metropolitan Council and Yorkshire Arts.

CONTENTS

9	Initiation
11	In the Farmyard
12	Children's Voices at Breakfast
13	Lifting
14	Family
15	Blue
16	The Cabbage Cutter
17	The Moon and the Fat Man
18	When I Died
19	Where Does the Dark Go?
20	What the Blind Man Sees
21	Fish
23	Church Window
24	Reflection in a Photograph
26	The Unicorn
27	Stag's Skull
28	The Artist Walks to Work
29	Bonnard: The Open Window
30	The Anatomy Lesson
31	Mandelstam
32	Shostakovitch
33	The Shape of Things
34	Sisyphus
35	Signs
36	Viola Weather
37	Morning
38	Absence
39	The Convenience of Bridges
41	In the Imperial War Museum
43	Arms
44	Removals
45	Holiday
46	Fear

47	Shells and Butterflies
48	Eurydice
49	Hackenback's Limp
50	Nag's Head, Cape Hateras
51	Montana de Oro Bay
52	Disney World
53	The Plan
54	Scrap
55	The Garden of Eden
56	Ark of the Covenant
57	Jacob's Ladder
58	Holding On
60	Cow
61	The Train
62	A Dream of Football
63	Dissolution

For my wife and children

Initiation

Egg

I am sitting in the dark. I am female.
I am about to roll. With my sisters I am waiting.
We are sitting in water, knocking softly against each other
like pebbles on a shore. The tumult reaches us
through glass, though glass and water and sisterhood
are not yet arrived. It is the faintest of movements in air,
thistledown, fairy wings, a dragon fly pulse.
We put down our mirrors that sit inside us.
Over our white faces we pull on the masks of gods.
We look disinterested. The air hums.
Our roundness smiles. Far off a thrashing of tails.

Sperm

In bathrooms and bedrooms all over suburbia
we gaze into mirrors. We are beside ourselves.
Waxing our hair and flexing our muscles,
we stare into the vacancy that is our eyes.
The sun sets like an oil slick. At one precise moment
all the street lights go on. We leave our front doors.
We will give of our best. One of us tonight
is the lucky one. Dark and forceful,
he won't take no for an answer. Eyes downcast,
she will swoon in her whiteness,
waiting for her bubble to burst.

Foetus

Lord of the startled heartbeat, naked Buddha.
Slumped in the juice of distraction. Thumb in mouth.
Lungs like deflated balloons. No questions asked.
Monotonous throbbing of pulses. Tadpole.
Nerves crawling through the body like spiders.
Your mother's expectant moon snagged in the branches.
Beyond the edges of the dark there is more dark.

There is the world of the unexpected.
Gravity will tip you suddenly upside down.
Before you know it, your perfect self
will slide slowly, effortlessly from you
like splinters of glass from a shattered mirror.
We will watch helplessly our broken reflections
in the pieces, unable to put them back.

In the Farmyard

Travelling the cow's backbone from rump to shoulder –
a bamboo ridge pole on rocky mounds;
slung under
a furry globe, the finger
tracing down latitudes of winter coat,
soft as a baby's hair;
the flat milk sack warm on the hand,
like a child's fever.
Four rubbery teats angled like chair legs;
pulling down melodies of milk
into a tin bucket.

Crossing the cobbled yard, laced
with flailed grains of oat and barley,
the cold rings in the ears, like a blacksmith's hammer,
freezing history into the senses. The midnight blue sow, pink saddled,
slumps on her side, exhausted, as though ridden there,
her eyes half closed with the ecstasy of sucking mouths.
One piglet detaches herself, navigates
the southern tip of trotter, the gulf of throat,
across the inlet of the mouth into the warm storm
of nostril, putting in, snuffling, at the ears,
before releasing herself
in a parabola of discovery,
reinventing the passage of her life.

My little daughter in her mother's arms
laughs like a chicken, asks,
'Are they eating her?'

Yes, they are eating her.

Children's Voices at Breakfast

The boy has silver hair, blue eyes and freckles.
He wears a New York Yankees baseball cap.
He draws cartoons of men with muscles like mountains.
He watches TV and thinks we go on and on for ever,
as he says, till we land up in heaven or hell.

The girl listens with her dark eyes.
The tea's brown tongue is licking out the cup,
she says, as if to nobody.

When you fold your memories in the map
of all the moments you have ever had,
the cup is stillness on your lips.
The words of children never counted much.
We shut them out. Yet it's for you alone
they give their silence up, to show you
something you will never have again.

Lifting

I lift my son, warm from his bed.
He is tall now, half my length,
and heavy in my arms.
Somnolent on tiptoe, he staggers,
penis erect, pisses. We listen to the sound
of water on water. He drops his head.

Back in my arms he slumps asleep.
He fits his body to my body.
I am a walking bed.
He could be comfortable in the branches of a tree.
He lifts his head, and manages
three words, Where, where, where?
Even in sleep he wants his mother.

In his bed he whispers me, goodnight,
and I return to kiss him,
but he is already gone.

Down the landing his baby sister wakes.
I go to her more willing than a lover,
more in demand. She roots for food,
her arm around my neck. I take her to her mother.

Family

No sun distils a midday mist hanging
from beech to beech. It spins a film of moisture
on our faces, that keeps us disengaged.
We sink in the accumulated scent of leaves.

In a fire's half light in the drawing room
eyes gleam in lazy conversation. Children
moon from one distraction to another.
The eight month baby in my lap looks
from family to flame, his eyes cold blue
and fascinated. Grasping the air up
like a curtain. His brain is brimmed with language.

So, in ember light in the evening we play
charades, and I get *Laughter in the Dark*.
I act the last word first.

Blue

Three blue bottles on a windowsill,
sunlight white on the rim, her velvet dress
thrown on the bed – a green snake skin sloughed off.
Everything bathed in elemental light.
Everything changed, washed off. The bed turned back.
The man who lowed and grunted like the beasts
and saw himself ridiculously a god –
she sees him in her telescope
the wrong way round. He's minuscule as moons.
Silk green lizards run up her body,
flick-flicking their tongues in the direction of her mouth.
Fat bodied grasshoppers drift across her eye line.
A skeletal bird pecks at her face.
Sometimes her anger is a box for crying in,
unfurling on a ribbon of song snatches
like clothes on a washing line –
'soft bellied love', 'slippery beauty'.
It itches and scratches her like brambles.
The delicate porcelain water jug
placates her, poisons leaching from her
down a stream that ends at these three bottles,
blue as blue against a varied sky.
The three blue poison bottles emptied of everything
but sunlight slanting on the window sill.

The Cabbage Cutter

Late afternoon of summer,
the thick, still air choked with remote voices.
Wood doves cooing, amorous feathered gods.
A man in shirt sleeves slams the door of a beat up car.
Coming from work, his tie undone. He saunters,
glances back at the road he's come along. Into the shop.

Propelled by his entrance, the mechanics of motion,
another man leaves by the back door. A grey-haired man
in heavy boots and shorts – brown legs, dark brown knees.
He walks down rows of black green savoys.
Astride one, he lops off the firm fresh head
with a kitchen knife. The cabbage squeals.
The first man stands on the front porch, oblivious,
hands in pockets, listening. He straightens up
with the other man's return. They exchange a few words.
He carries the head triumphantly, tosses it on the back seat.

Dust rises. The hedgerow snatches at it.
The dead returned as birds settle their wings.
There is a murmuring in the air,
as if something undreamed of has finally happened.

The Moon and the Fat Man

Under a full moon wind ruffles grass tussocks.
New lambs frantically seeking on moonlit fells.
Irregular hills jag the dark skyline.

Across from here the fat man fills the lighted window,
sits sideways at table, eating in dungarees.
By day he grows potatoes in neat rows –
green tops muddied, hanging for the water
he brings in buckets. Fat and thoughtful in dungarees.
Lifted up here, all there is to do is eat them.

How far the lambs' cries carry on the wind.
The fat man cocks his ear, stops chewing,
lays down his fork beside his plate,
his face three quarter silhouette.
How close the moon. How deep the wet roots.

When I Died

When I died, it was a beginning.
My body was washed down by a woman
with rubber gloves on her elegant fingers.
I watched her remotely. She hesitated
over my penis. The air around me smiled.
I was free, my heart resting at last.
My sphincters took a holiday. I flew out
somewhere, last minute, fast as light.

My dog moped in his basket. My wife awake
all night, the dark full of voices.
I called from huge distances. My children heard
and turned their pale faces to the window.
The wind threw handfuls of rain at the glass.
Year on year the trees whispered away their leaves.

Where Does the Dark Go?

Darkness brings everything closer, hand in glove,
a word in the ear. Horizons disappear.
Distant trains scissor off the edge of town,
run their cold wheels along your cheek bone.

Lovers push darkness back into each other,
though it seeps out through half closed eyes.
It rolls around the throat like thunder,
the tongue a swollen corpse in a sacred river.
Exhausted, they fall back into it and drown.

On clear, still nights in winter snow turns blue,
and the cock crow breaks off pieces of silence.
You will see fires flare in the charcoal sky.

When dawn comes, the dark is taken down,
and folded into thick green woods, where foxes
gnaw at it all day, mistaking it for carrion.

What the Blind Man Sees

What is this space? Nothing? Emptied of light,
the night still has its stars, or darker clouds.
Visited by angels, angelic forms
of light, high mountains of illumination,
but inside the head. Not the last white light of dying,
but diffuse glimmer of palpitating wings.

Endorphin angels? I've seen them on mountains.
In the valley where a ribbon of white water
tumbles into a green pool, liquid lines of sheep
flowing across fells. High above them, seraphic bodies
as far as the eye can see, filling the imagined sky,
taking over from this darkness, emptied of light.

Fish

We drove into the Welsh hills above Llandovery –
lines of headstones propped against the chapel walls,
as if workmen were digging up the past.

We camped in a triangle of grass between road and river.
From tent to car we tied a rope that guided me,
guided my first footsteps into the dark.
You were learning to be a blind man's wife,
to read tombstone names to me in my darkness.

In those days the least excursion took me hours,
summoning the courage from somewhere to stumble and be stared at.

On the second morning you were tidying the ground,
and must have from the corner of your eye caught
the bright leap of the fish. I heard it –
and saw it too in my mind's eye, upright,
arching its iridescent back, the eye fixed
blindly on the direction it was taking.
We shared what we had seen. My eye as valid as yours.
Later you coaxed me naked into a deep pool,
where the river had piled up boulders and damned itself,
feeling with my feet for rock holds in the clear water, down
and all the way under. My eyes ached with cold.
I leaped back, clearing my shoulders with a whoop.

Later, you, pregnant, lying on your side,
I loved the touch of your tightening skin, breasts bulging with milk,
your heavy belly flattened on the ground.
Round and round my hands went. Suddenly the baby kicked
and rose like a fish in a river. I almost caught him.
He must have hung there in the amniotic fluid
like a fish hovering against the flow, listening,
waiting and waiting on heart beat, hearing our distant voices.

When he came out of you, he mewed like a cat,
and someone placed him in my arms, wrapped in paper.
I stared blindly into the crack he made in time.
Someone turned on a tap. Now at a bus stop
he is a moon to a cluster of girls,
a young bull with school bag hunched against the rain.

You and I in a quiet time sit wondering.
The clock from the Llandovery farmhouse hangs
on the wall and booms the hours away.
The room fills with silence as the river fills endlessly,
endlessly cleaning itself, waiting for fish to jump.

Church Window

A blind man looks at a photograph

Your hand on mine moves mine from side to side
across the photograph. In one corner
hang cobwebs, sagging under the unseen
weight of age. Our hands, like coupling spiders,
examining the candid rectangle
of church window. A lengthened cross divides
panes of clear glass. Paint peels from the recess,
where dead carnations in a stone vase turn
to dust.

      This broken moment where we focus
in hand and eye all our expectation.
Beyond the rectangle, beyond the cross,
beyond the desiccating, flaking stone,
my finger traces suddenly a crest
of hill descending like your collar bone.

Reflection in a Photograph

You look at me – a silver nitrate ghost
floating in the alchemy of words.
You gaze back down the road you have come along,
back towards that little, ordinary, cocky girl,
propped there in party dress before the camera.
Born, as they said, half bird, your wings clipped
painfully in plastic, itched and comforted
by women, enrolled into mythologies
of wings and preciousness and incompletenesses
by storytellers we never asked to speak.
Afraid to let you fly, they taught you how to fall.

Never asked to be born, we were always here,
watching and wondering and being gawped at.
Because I couldn't see, they couldn't see me.

You are my mirror. You give me back my body
in the space between us, made of voice and emptiness,
of difference and commonality.
I am lost and found in your reflection.

What are we waiting for – anybody, nobody?
Always and already, we start from here.
We were told by ghost voices long ago,
there was one body, one mind, one way of being whole.
I was that anxious boy wondering if it was true.
And somewhere on that sudden road from childhood,
where mouths dropped open when we dared to pass,
I learned we live in many bodies – breath body,
breast body, tongue, mouth, cunt body, holy body, **dream body**.
But some body chose this body to carve
their negligence and nightmares on.
We learned to be lonely at heart, and from the heart

emerging slowly, little by little,
leg, foot, breast, thigh, eyes, voice – a hand opening
finger by finger, palm up, offering what we had to give.
No need to call the tune. We always were the tune.

How beautiful, described to me, your nakedness,
however wrapped in perspex fantasy.
Your wholeness makes me whole.
Not winged but grounded womanhood, whose gaze
must shame us out of myths of imperfection.
We have come a long way, and are here now,
burning, crowned in flame.
No weather in the world can blow us down.

The Unicorn

After Rainer Maria Rilke

This is the one of uncertain existence
who lingered timidly in Eden,
and never wandered out along their path of knowledge;
yet they invested her in flesh –
upright, silk necked, loose flanked,
and, caught in her shimmering gaze, they loved her.

Desire howled for her,
when they glimpsed her on the edge of battle,
Gideon's angel, nonchalant under the oak;
or, reflected in the priest's bright chalice
lifted in smoking candle light;
or, when other, impatient angel's creaked their wings
above them, sweat on their side curls, she entered
their emptiness, raising her gentle head,
hesitant on the threshold of existence.

They fed her not on grain,
but on the possibility of being,
and in itself this gave her such pure strength,
she grew miraculously a horn,
a single horn, out of her forehead.

She carried her own soft whiteness willingly to them,
and, fixed in their silvered mirror, walked
innocently into it,
moving silkily, ambiguously deep inside.

Stag's Skull

Turn the photo round – the angle falsifies:
out of a shaded cranny an owl's head
watches us. Round again – the old stag's skull,
big as a rock, the fault line visible.
Antlers sawn off, cropped to the bone,
that must have swelled and steepled like a tree.
He'd lock them knocking in a rutting drive,
or shake them, grunting hugely at the moon.

Mute now, he's lit dramatically for you
to trigger off your death defying shots,
studioed and studied for the sake of art –
a form with abstract possibilities:
though captive, penitent, cut down to size,
still menacing, still poised, still imminent.

The Artist Walks to Work

Along this simple avenue of trees
the painter, shirt and easel, hat and shadow,
strides to work. His nonchalant straw hat,
his devil-may-care trousers. The distant hills
give up their blueness, the corn its yellow.

I walk this white imagined road, dust on my shoes,
dreaming the artist under artless cypresses.
Sit in purple fields at dusk among almond shells.

I trace the road to Mont Saint Victoire –
the map on the studio wall had shown it,
under gigantic, shivering plane trees.
There is no visionary mountain. I look everywhere.
All I find is a dry well and corn stubble.

Late in the indigo evening I meet the artist,
those inconsolable eyes, on the undiscoverable road.

Bonnard: The Open Window

In this room you sleep the sleep of the dead,
your old head on blue canvass.
Dreams steal to you in cat silence.

The window opens on greenness
like a new thought. The tree touches
the translucent blue of vast distances.

A blue vase is a handful of sky:
the shutters and the dark blind a camera.
The cat moves her head ambiguously.

This blue, this wide, infinite air
holds the window open one long moment,
while you sleep the sleep that fills the room.

The Anatomy Lesson

In the underground car park three black men take the keys.
Two don't speak English. They offer to wash the car.
In the cave mouth you look at the opulent arch
of the bird cage Opera House. Heads down in the rain,
still smiling, ears ringing with the German syllables
of Mozart. The corporate clients make their way
to where flunkies hold the car door open
for a quick getaway. In a tenement block
a black woman carries washing in a basket
to the launderette. BMWs cruise past with smoked windows.

Men in black tail coats frozen in candle light
around the dissecting table frown with authority.
The surgeon peels back the layers of the dead woman.
They have come from a dinner party, the opera, the theatre.
In the limelight of science they stare at the mise-en-scène
of the woman's open womb. They are expecting the moon,
but the moon has taken herself away behind clouds.
Instead one has arranged a foetus in a jar
with beads. White as a pickled egg. A pickled moon.
Down the corridor we watch the simulated movements
of hysterics. Real leather ovary compressors.
A padded jacket keeps the body straight.

I am a blind man. A man living on the streets asks
if we are lost. For a few pennies he can show us.
Show us what? I shrug my shoulders. What is there to see?

Mandelstam

> 'Nobody has said they actually saw Osip dead. Nobody
> claims to have washed the body or put it in the grave.
> I can be certain of only one thing, that somewhere
> Osip's suffering ended in death.'

After the rocking horse headlamps of the car,
the dream of forests, the misty river crossing,
the stammering interment of the sun,
the upstart poet wakes and watches. His senses
stick to nothing, the face framed in the window,
fixed, discharged, disintegrating, open,
reiterating the rhythm of the journey,
the space around him crowded with betrayal:
a hero from nowhere rattling into exile
under the hard, articulate, calm, bright stars.
He knows the worm, that winters in the Veronesh hills,
will plough its bloodless furrow in his brain.

Here at the co-ordinates of breathlessness and death
they take from him his coat, his shirt, his boots.
He gives them back the black words from his throat.
They stand around frozen to what he knows.

She holds the emptiness in her crooked arm.
Dreams wake her. She wraps herself in hope.
She writes, 'My beloved, far-away sweetheart,
I have no words to write this letter to you;
I send it into an empty space.
It is me, Nadya; where are you?'

He takes the hills, the sky,
the kiss of separation,
and puts them on for clothes.
He shakes his head,
and from it fall diamonds.

Shostakovitch

Boldly
he seeks
from the rostrum
the face of the ruling clique.
His tight mouth refuses their nostrum.
His black eyes
speak.

In front of the smiling players
he bows like a skittery horse,
his eye brows arched in question marks
over the wild applause.

His questions hang like rags on wire,
like skin on bone,
like souls on fire.

Slowly
he searches the faces
that burn in the edge of the light.
Amazement
washes him clean as a corpse.
His cheek is ashen white.

He tangles himself in dilemma,
in the minutes and hours of doubt.
Wrapped like a drowning swimmer in water,
he is snagged like a hook in a trout.
They love him.
They won't let him out.

The Shape of Things

Euclid saw it. It hung there
for a moment in front of him,
came and went. Its sides were sheer.
A kite in the cerebral air.
Euclid tugged on the string. The shape moved.
He saw the lines of its sides, its angles, its corners.
Drew it in sand. Rubbed it out with his foot.
Started again. Over and over.
The memory of it stuck to his toes.
Entered the tips of his fingers.
He had never seen anything so straight and true.
Always his shapes had been breasts or moonlight,
softly rounded, somewhere to sleep in,
to collide with. But this shape was distant.
In the head, away from the body.
It thrilled him with its absolute edges.
Euclid saw it hovering before him –
the ghost of an idea.

Sisyphus

Not one for myths, Sisyphus. Carry on like this,
he'll have himself in history. Breathes heavy,
mouth full of stone-dust. You'd think he'd get it
second time around, third, fifth, ad infinitum.
Maybe, if he pushes long and hard enough,
this boulder takes off and walks the rest itself.
He'd stand there sweating, wondering what he'd done.

You might suppose Newton would be wise to it,
first time he dropped his trousers by mistake.
He wasn't thinking straight, eyes full of stars,
other fish to fry. What did he do?
Double locked them with a belt or two.

It seems the moment has to bring itself to being.
When questions hit you on the head. Now gravity's
the order of the day. Pushing against it's the thing.

Night falls. Man falls. Walls come tumbling down.
One law to govern everything? Words fall
between us. We never seem to learn,
or learn too late, as rocks fly past our ears,
we must imagine Sisyphus is happy.

Signs

When Jacques Derrida came, we went to hear,
aimless in inarticulate pursuit
of wisdom, dapper in its tie and suit,
that made the ground beneath us disappear,
a sense of disconnection taking root.

My half deaf friend stood up to make a point.
Derrida didn't understand his drift,
and, seeking signs, began to search his face.
They stood in limbo like the desert saints.
I watched Derrida knot his tie and lift
one hand, as if delivering a grace.

Viola Weather

This is viola weather. Wakes the house
to haunting. Wind punches windows. Doors settle.
A gangling dog slumps thumping on the floor.
Stranded in armchairs, wind waves lapping
round the walls. Rain squalls chaotic grains.
I am nerve ends. Mister Stevens rainy man.

Daydream – a dialogue with time. The old way out.
One bound and he was free. No trains going my way
on empty, soot flaked stations. Greatcoated,
pockets stuffed with paperbacks, twenty something,
all coat and elbows, hunched over coffee cups.
Aluminium doors swoons shut after a passenger.
I'm reading *Herzog*. I remember the name!
I lasso the moment from the comfort of middle age
books kept me warm. I was blanketed in print.
Cafeteria staff in green aprons.
Was that the colour? Did coffee taste like that?
The memories call out from that dangerous moment,
the cigarette gesture, look avoiding looks,
steam trains hissing on other empty platforms,
a book's title, waiting. Did I ever leave?
A train whistle out of the station tunnel –
the long, slow, steady, low, held note of a viola.

Morning

I am
a stranger stepping from a train,
dragging the baggage of night behind him,
flat footed
on the platform, waiting for someone,
anyone, to receive him into their language.
I plunge my hands in water,
and fill with sadness
from a place so far away
not even memory can travel there.

My daughter,
whose little history
contains two winters only,
doesn't see the shadow in the mirror,
that arrived by night, says, amazed,
'You're making a slide on your face'.
I smile for the first time.

On the street
the sun touches my ear, my shoulder,
like an old friend not needing conversation.
The boy beside me laughs.
He has seen the moon still hanging in the sky –
a half forgotten, half remembered face,
a lamp left burning overnight
for unexpected visitors.

Absence

At night the streets are rolled up,
and the houses stacked neatly away.

The wind walks down off the hill,
lifts the roof with one finger, to see if I am in.

Shadows shrug their tall shoulders.
Chairs shrink like spiders into dark corners.

Dogs look to rattled windows, alert as priests,
while pale dolls weep softly into their sheets.

The dead walk past deep in conversation.
They walk absently into sleep's open mouth.

By morning everything is back in place.
I step in a spillage of sunlight.
A blackbird flies singing from the water tap.

The Convenience of Bridges

1

We are full of bridges.
The bridge you see over your shoulder on a dark night
and can never find again. Nightmare bridge.
The beautiful white bridge in the middle of dream lake
nobody sets foot on.

The grandfather takes the child by the hand to the bridge.
But they never cross it. She never wonders why.
It is embedded. Look, that's where you have to go!

The old bridge upstream stretched as far as it could.
It took itself to the middle and stopped,
the unworked edge of stone still visible.
The bridge that takes you half way over
and disappears under your feet.

He was doing so well, building as he walked.
Did he fall mid stream into the tidal water?
Or did he keep on walking, walking on air?

2

Something stopped the grandfather stepping onto the bridge.

People speak of death as the crossing of bridges.
The untroubled walk to the unknown country.
The crossing of t's and the dotting of i's.

We don't remember the days of the turbulent current,
unpacified pain, the fear of not paying the ferryman enough,
so he spits on his hands and rows out in the stream, cursing.

We take ourselves conveniently across bridges.

Death is the bridge swept away from under us.
Now, only now, you put your foot on it gingerly,
the parapet under your fingers. You make the first move.

In the Imperial War Museum

In a letter
handwriting sprawls, off duty, teeters
on the brink.
Ink fading into washed out sky. The weft
of paper lifted with neglect
and damp,
the regimental stamp. Folds opening
like lungs hinged to lost words.

Stink of fibreglass trench under the simulated bluster of guns
                                              that thump
  the underside of imaginary clouds.
  Rag hair under a tin hat unnerves the touch.
  Rats in plastic hiatus on the rim
  like held breath composing platitudes
  to dampen down the fear,
  here and at home.
  These fabricated reconstructions –
  static as narrated dreams,
  not the crawling, warm, wet pulp of nightmare.
  Terror lashed down by tedium.

What we think, he doesn't talk about –
out there, waterlogged, mud encrusted, under
thunder clogged skies. Up
and over into metal rain. Horses
like plough teams struggling in flooded furrows.
What he knows about death
is nailed upside down to a fence, crow's wing
flapping in gusts,
slack necked, the crystallised eyes
like shattered ice.

Burst wounds of fading words scrawled across page
after page of ordinary details
that ambush our outrage. The real guns
are rusted, silent. These words
boom
and boom.

Arms

After the blast only the eye is calm.
I don't care who it was, I know it's done –
a rocket in a block of flats and one
man walking blind, his dead child in his arms.

A zealot's eye, the cold butt on the palm:
some finger pulled the trigger on the gun,
some boy, some man, some fucking mother's son.
This girl is any daughter; ours his arms.

In quiet pools of sexual regret
we never think that murder is the plan,
that we were born to do each other harm.
You'd think you'd see it once and not forget.
You couldn't wish it on another man –
the vacant eye, the empty, aching arms.

Removals

A man on the stairs glances over his shoulder,
holding a painting. It's the look spring gives to winter.
A woman in T-shirt and jeans fills the doorway.

There's a man with my name in the room stirring paint.
The walls wait blankly in smears of thin sunlight.
A desk lies dismantled on uncarpeted flooring,
its papers bagged in bin-liners, ready to go.

A girl stands at the window. Sunlight plaits her hair.
Thoughts spill like coloured beads over the sill.
Her brother, hair like corn, dawdles by the table.
Days trail him the way he leaves clothes where they fall.

The girl turns. The boy stares beyond her at the wall.
The woman, arms akimbo, distracted in the room's centre.
 Front door open, they are carrying out the last picture.

Holiday

We took a walk every evening,
the light binding us in fine threads,
to look out to sea, the far, bright sea.
Father in new daps. Mother with coat wrapped round her,
me, 15, captive in chains of mother love.
We stood shivering in shop doorways eating chips,
before we turned in at the bed and breakfast.
Nothing was ever quite right for my mother,
my dad always trying to make it so.
We sat on a sweltering pebble beach
on plastic lilos with another family.
I wanted other eyes on me, other words.
The weather was wonderful, the sea, deep,
and we were only an hour from home.

Fear

Somewhere it crawled into me –
a rat in a pipe, so that,
when the children come in laughing
from the garden, I know
they will never come that way again.

A child myself by the makeshift hen house
of tea chests, roof felt and chicken wire,
I stood watching those fussy little women
come peck pecking towards me
in their drab, brown, puritan dresses
and blood soaked neckerchiefs.

Above me a grim face I call 'Father',
his hand like blue cheese on the axe handle.

The chickens are long dead,
their carcasses, half built cathedrals,
congealed on the kitchen table.
The hand is empty at father's side.
But still the fear resides
in rooms of nervous, scratchy women,
who come at me with their beady eyes.

Or, dreaming in the dead of night, I fall
like a mason's mallet from a wooden tower
under the high leaf-fringed vaulting, leaving only
chiselled faces, stone eyeballs, uncompleted smiles.

Shells and Butterflies

She told him she was a student of optometrics,
as she walked him down the long corridor.
When they turned the corner, she put his hand
on her breast. Her nipple looked like a pink shell,
but it didn't feel like a shell at all.
Later he ran his hands down her belly –
butterfly wings on the thick shrub of hair.

He didn't know, whether to love her or collect her.
He took out his pin, inserted it deftly,
felt for the flesh, withdrew it, sucked the brine
through his teeth, careful not to spill a drop.

He took photographs of her body,
some close up, others from the edge of space,
her breast the shape of Columbus' world,
her wedge of hair an arrowhead flying towards him.

When they were developed, he put them away
in a drawer, forgot them. But sometimes,
deep inside him, a butterfly stirred, kicked
off her chrysalis and spread her wings over him.

When he died, someone went to see him,
and came back saying he looked like an empty shell.
But she knew where he was. She went looking for him
like a butterfly walking on a dried pool,
searching in the mud cracks with her proboscis,
sometimes opening and closing her wings,
shimmering her soft sea-shell colours.

Eurydice

I remember everything perfectly,
shaken out of the day's consciousness
like loose change from a dead man's pocket.
Last night I went down into sleep's subway,
half empty carriages rattling past.
You stood on the platform with your mother,
looking in my direction. I whistled for you.
You weren't listening. Your hair was corn stubble,
your breasts the burial chambers of anonymous kings.
I was the archaeologist of desire.

The train doors closed like a scallop shell.
Your blackbird mother called you back to her,
and pulled a veil of evening over your fields.

I jangled on into the sleeping suburbs,
where leaves curl like lips, sardonically,
at this ridiculous self I wear –
sliding on frozen oceans in dancing shoes,
the melody unravelling like a bandage.

Now, in the middle of a conversation,
a mouth is a crumpled skirt, or subway doors
opening and closing, far, far away,
saying, 'Speak to me!' When it is too late.

Hackenback's Limp

Let me tell you the story of Hackenback's limp.
He was wired up cruelly from ankle to knee
to God knows where, and he crawled on all fours,
or so Magda says. Can we go for a walk?
Oh, I'd love to, but Lulu is waiting
to show us her bike. It's years since I saw you.
I promised her mother. I wanted to ask you
about your affairs. I don't want to make love,
not try to recapture what wasn't there then.
What happened to you? Is Hackenback yours?
And how many children did you manage to have?
Are you still with that man? I hear him most nights.
He seems to know so much about everything,
I feel quite unable to cope. Do you think about me?
I went blind, but you know that. I wrote you a letter.
I imagine you send all your children to school.
Like the rest of your set, the coffee and concerts,
the smart conversation, the conference seasons.
Is this envy or longing I feel? I can't tell.
And would we still speak the same language as then?
Let's go for a walk. The rest are asleep.
It's warm, and you're wearing a dress like the one
you had on on the day we put in at the islands.
The cliffs were hunched over like scribes at a desk.
Oil trailed on the water like manuscript drawings.
It was then that you mentioned the eyes of the poet.
We had travelled all night in the face of the moon.
The stars were alive. Your short hair was tousled.
Boats were put down. We clambered on board,
steadied by hands that reached up like beggars.
The wake of the water behind us was burning.
You've not led me before. I'm quite good on rocks.
And I want you to tell me all that you've felt.
It's sunny and warm and Lulu can wait.
You can start, if you like, with Hackenback's limp.

Nag's Head, Cape Hateras

There were three of us in the tent. I was
delirious. Stepping outside to piss,
the night wrapped me in mosquitoes. I was
a silk sheet covered in loose stitches.
The moon hung there – an unenamelled tooth.

Next day they took the inner tent for shade.
It was an oven on the beach. I cooked.
Deliriously I did handstands in the surf
to cool my head. I was a virgin sailor,
before he walked out, musket in hand,
across the Hateras swamps, claiming the land.

In the motel I drank eight pints of water,
and slept three days. They sat by the pool,
reading like strangers in an airport lounge.

Montana de Oro Bay

Where the headland cliff drops like a stone into the sea,
carved from black rock,
a solitary cloaked mourner, round shouldered in silhouette.
The dark, still presence disturbs its wings
like a broken umbrella. A cormorant
watching sea splintering over shelves of shale
along the cluttered shore line.

Now we hang like watery birds of prey
over our own slow moving, unsuspecting shadows.

Two hundred years ago holy intruders anchored here
in the bay. Hauling down swords and bibles.
They shaded their eyes against the climbing sun,
watched a gang of cormorants like poised pall bearers
on the rocks, examining disruptions in the depths.
They saw Chumash canoes ride the galloping waves
to meet them, weighed down with Abalone shells,
low in the water, while, far beyond them,
Californian Poppies turned the hills to gold.

Disney World

I dream of eating pink ice cream through keyholes,
bank roles of notes that flicker like Victorian porn
on windy piers – What The Butler Failed To See.
I dream of lift shafts, holes in the ground,
water levels rising and men with grainy faces
staring sidelong at the camera.

In the daylight I ransack books of poems
for film names, production companies,
trailer blurbs and poster slogans.
My secretary brings me a coffee to my desk.
She sprawls across it, half undressed, her breasts
flattened on the shiny surface. Watching
the loose curl on her neck, I'm the King of the Jungle.
The air conditioning hums. The rubber plant droops.
I write in duplicate my expense account.

The Plan

You always had a plan. A plan for living in –
a job, a wife, a three-bedroomed house. Every time
you came home, you propped it up against the table lamp,
made small adjustments with a pencil stub,
checked your bank statements. Your wife grew big.
That was the plan. One night she didn't take the pill
and you were flying. Right up until the birth,
the birthing room and everything. Everything
was right – the scan, the baby-grow, the time.
You held her hand and heard the baby cry.
It cried and cried and never looked like stopping.

Now if you tease her, she screams. She's fourteen.
In all those years you had to find it out.
She's never planned a thing. Even the psychologist
was lost. They put her here because they didn't know
what else to do. She doesn't know how old she is.
She wanders round the room inspecting moments
and then dropping them. She's never held a pencil,
never made a plan, and never will.
You'll do it for her till your time is up.

Scrap

She's done the round of class, learned to assert
herself. Slogans come tumbling from her mouth.
Don't bother her with maps! She's heading out.
It's you have failed. You're scrap. You're obsolete.

She wants her friends to change. She's dyed her hair.
She'll sometimes nail you with her anecdotal youth,
and stub out failure under her bare feet.
Success demands a distance from the truth.

We wait with bated breath to hear whose fault
her life is next. Accept you're in retreat.
Her soup's gone cold. She's eyeing the dessert.

The Garden of Eden

You feel it crawling at your feet. The pressure drops.
The temperature that steadied once begins to bend.
The air is clammy at your throat. You hadn't noticed
layer on layer of meaning building up. Nobody told you.
Nobody was there, or so you thought. This summer idyll
coming to an end, before it had begun.
You were surprised by unleashed whispers, cool breezes
like a child's breath. And as for her enchantment,
it was the spell of childhood. Childhood, that is,
until she dropped her dress. You watched her hand up-arching
secretly in shadow, gloved in apple leaves.
The loosened breast. She looked at you.
You filled her eye. Her mouth was wet.

Ark of the Covenant

Think of the poor sods who carried the Ark of the Covenant.
They put it at the far end of the Temple
among the pomegranates, bulls and date-palms,
a place for God to live. Imagine,
standing all day in the presence of God, so close
you can hear him breathe. You carry this heavy thing
from place to place, wondering what it is
you are carrying. You feel it move,
adjust its position. Your knees buckle.
Your need for meaning heavy as a hollowed tree.
You carry it from place to place, because you have no choice.

Jacob's Ladder

First, there was the wrestle with the angel –
just like being in the womb with *him* again,
that delicious smell of love and danger,
up till the angel kicked me in the groin.

I grew smooth, cautious, planed along the grain,
avoiding knots, looking for the angle:
my first born brother innocent as rain,
headlong, God's fool, a cup without a handle.

After I did the dirty on my dad,
the flat, ungiving desert suited me.
The ladder in the clouds was all I had.
The hurricane of power uprooted me.

Lying, restless, on stones gives you a hard head.
I signed a contract with the Living God.

Holding On

We found my sister's grave sunk in the ground.
'3-in,' my father said, and he was right –
a man too old to reckon where he is
from day to day. A bleak and empty place.

The traffic climbed the long slow hill to town –
everybody going somewhere fast.
We straggled, almost nonchalant with expectation.
My mother walked ahead into the past.

The grave was there, cheap marble pulled apart,
as if the ground had trembled from the hurt.
I thought it was the wind caught in my coat –
my earth bound mother sobbing down the years.

Workmen had laid skewed slabs of concrete on the grave,
as if to keep her in, to keep her down.
She wasn't there. I stood imagining the bones.
My father walked away just like he always did.

My mother never saw him cry; but once
she caught him in the shed, head bowed,
his dirty hands, his shoulders shaking,
putting all my sister's books and clothes in order.

My mother said she saw her on the stairs,
and then she lived with us forever –
a happy, gentle, bookish girl of ten.
She must have thought that all of time was hers.

 I watched my father rearrange the stones,
still strong enough to lift and drop and lift.
My mother put fresh flowers in the pot
– and so we left her.

Is this a life? Imagined ways of being,
a few old clothes, bones, and a ceaseless wind;
a girl remembered in a marble cage,
sorrow still kicking after all these years?

Cow

Mother, there's a cow in the front garden.
She's eating the Rowan tree,
and the postman won't come in.

A crowd is gathering in the street.
A police car is pulling up,
its blue light flashing.

Look, Mother, they are coming up the path,
a rope halter in their hands.
They're knocking at the front door.

They're asking me questions, Mother.
Who am I? What shall I say my name is?

Say 'Moo' dear, just say 'Moo'.

They're leading me away, a rope round my neck.
Somebody with soft hands is putting a hood over my head.

Can you still see the cow, dear? Can you still see the cow?

The Train

My father sits impassively and I, opposite,
mirroring his silence. The two women speak.
A spellbound tiredness wraps me in spider threads.
My mind the desert of a poem. Nothing to say.
My mother is struggling with a resolution she cannot find.
The years have drifted past, and now she can't remember,
or won't remember, who and what, and will not answer why.
Like passengers in a railway carriage
that no longer exists – the facing seats,
the leather window strap, the maps of England behind the heads,
watching a landscape washed in smoke and sunlight racing by.

There in the waterlogged meadow stands the girl.
The hedges hung with spiders' webs that flutter
like Tibetan prayer flags. Someone took a razor to the sky.
Alone, with her camera focused on the retreating train.

My father is silent, as he always is,
and soon the women fall silent too,
and I only say, 'It's time to go'.

A Dream of Football

Three ghosted men play football in a dream,
my mother's brothers and my Dad. One dead,
one rich – green Mercedes with a special plate,
and my 90 year old father, playing football
in the wooden slatted, green felted garage
of my boyhood. They are all my age now.
The garage as it was, timeless, falling down,
windows held in by rusty nails, putty cracked.
My dad, bow-legged like Stanley Matthews, shoots.
The ball and my uncle crash into the window,
a zig zag crack the length of it. They stand guiltily,
Giacometti figures in a concrete landscape.
They look like boys. They laugh. They have come alive.
They are and are not there. As if death was only a dream
or a memory. As if life was a dream. Three men my age,
all boyish fears, all happy in their manliness.
I watch them now, as I did then.
Unable to join in. Waiting my turn.

Dissolution

The body will fall somewhere, a dropped ice cream
out of a child's hand. A frozen estuary
to an invisible sea. Occasional wasps.
Colours leached out. What remains is a stain,
the slow erosion of recognition.

You think by asserting you take a hold,
but your throat swells up. Nobody listens.
The words get squeezed and never spoken.

You're here because they tell you you are something,
but nothing is graspable. Your children
are old enough to stay away from home.
You sleep in their beds secretly in the night,
imagine them asleep; you even dream their dreams,
while the silence in your throat is melting.